Mercury Island

by Carmel Reilly

illustrated by Ian Forss

OXFORD
UNIVERSITY PRESS
AUSTRALIA & NEW ZEALAND

One day in winter, Dad came home from work looking very happy. "Guess what?" he said. "I've won first prize in the work raffle — a week away at Mercury Island!"

"Great!" replied Mum. "A tropical holiday is just what we need."

"Start packing," said Dad. "We leave next week."

"Hooray!" shouted Pippa and Eddie.

On the day they were leaving, everyone was very excited. Dad had a list of everything they needed to take.

"Now, have we got hats and sunscreen and shorts and t-shirts and boogie boards and ..."

"Yes," said Mum. "We've got everything. And Nanna's coming over to look after Star. Let's go. We have to catch our flight."

They were almost at the freeway when
Eddie asked, "Dad, did you pack the footy?"

"It's in my brown bag," said Dad.

"Brown bag?" said Mum. "I don't
remember loading a brown bag."

Dad pulled over, got out
of the car and opened the
boot. "Oh, no!" he cried.
"I left my brown
bag behind."

By the time they'd gone home to pick up Dad's bag, they were running very late.

When they got to the airport, they parked the car, grabbed their bags out of the boot and raced across to the terminal.

"Listen!" shouted Eddie when they were inside the terminal. "They're calling our names."

They ran to the check-in counter to check in their luggage and to get their boarding passes. Then they went through the security area and rushed to the departure gate.

"We've been waiting for you," said the man at the departure gate crossly.

The plane pulled out on to the runway.

"Phew!" said Dad. "Now we can relax."

As the plane took off, Pippa looked out the window. "Everything looks so small!" she said.

Eddie looked out, too. "There's our street," he said. "Wave to Star and Nanna!"

A few hours later, the plane started to land.

"Good, we're almost there," said Dad.

"It says here we have a short stopover on the way," said Mum.

"A stopover?" said Dad.

"It's only an hour," said Mum. "Just enough time to stretch our legs at the airport."

During the stopover, Mum and Pippa went to the airport cafe. Eddie and Dad decided to look around the airport.

"I didn't know this airport was so big," said Dad. "There are so many shops."

"Look at the toys in this shop!" said Eddie.

"And look at these games," said Dad.

9

Back at the cafe, Mum and Pippa heard the boarding call for their flight.

"Where are Dad and Eddie?" asked Pippa.

"We'll have to go and look for them," said Mum, looking at her watch.

FLIGHT MA001 IS NOW BOARDING

"I can't see them!" said Mum.

"I can't see them, either!" said Pippa.

FINAL BOARDING CALL FOR THE WILSON FAMILY, FLIGHT MA001

In the gift shop, Dad heard the final boarding call. "That's us!" he shouted, so loudly that everyone in the shop turned around.

Pippa heard Dad, too. "Is that you, Dad?" she called.

"Yes, we're in here!" yelled Eddie.

Mum, Dad, Eddie and Pippa raced to the boarding gate, down the ramp and on to the plane.

As they fell into their seats and snapped on their seatbelts, Dad sighed. "After all that running around, I'm going to need this holiday. Lots of sunshine will be great. Mercury Island, here we come!"

Then the pilot's voice came over the speakers.

"Welcome to Mercury Winter Resort," he said. "There's just been some snowfall and the weather is sunny – perfect for skiing and snowboarding."

"Winter resort?" said Dad looking puzzled. Mercury Island is supposed to be hot."

"This is Mercury *Resort* not Mercury Island," said Eddie pointing out the window. "It's definitely not hot!"

"Oh dear," said Mum. Pippa just giggled.

"It wasn't quite what we expected, but I don't think this holiday has turned out too badly," said Dad.

"I've always wanted to go snowboarding!" said Eddie.